MAINE WINDJAMMER CRUISES

Keeping the Tradition Alive

A Pictorial History of Maine's Original Windjammer Fleet

by Captain Ray Williamson

ISBN: 978-0-615-48385-6

Designed by Rich Eastman

Printed in China

5   4   3   2   1

Library of Congress Cataloging-in-Publication Data available upon request

Cover photo of *Grace Bailey* by Neal Parent

Acknowledgments

I would like to thank Rod Swift, who never tired of my endless questions about his father's company. His preservation of historic articles and photographs, along with company records and other documents, is responsible for most of the facts in this book. I am also deeply indebted to Captains Doug and Linda Lee, who allowed me to put a microscope on this small segment of their vast maritime archives.

Special thanks to Les and Ann Bex for access to their collection and the many opportunities they gave me when I first came to Camden. Thanks to the Penobscot Marine Museum and the Camden Historical Society for taking such a strong interest in preserving the heritage this company represents to the area and our maritime traditions in general.

Thank you to every photographer whose work I have been able to locate and regrets to those I have not. Thank you to every journalist who has ever written about Maine Windjammer Cruises, not only for preserving the history, but for their part in the success of this business.

It is with great appreciation that I acknowledge the long hours and timeless commitment of Margaret Jones, my personal assistant, who enthusiastically took on this project while continuing to manage the office and handle reservations.

Thanks to Jim Butler, my editor, for his patience and encouragement, and to Rich Eastman, who developed such a wonderful design.

Warmest appreciation to my wife, Ann, for her never-ending support and final edits.

Thank you to the captains and crews, too numerous to mention, whose dedication and commitment have preserved this way of life.

Finally, endless thanks go out to all of the "Old Salts," the passengers—past and present—who provide the cargo that give these vessels purpose. They are ultimately responsible for the continued existence of these windjammers.

To Ann, whose love and encouragement

have turned dreams into reality.

Introduction

In December 2010, Captain Ray Williamson contacted me about the book you hold in your hands; he was writing it to commemorate the 75th anniversary of Maine Windjammer Cruises, the company Captain Frank Swift (my father) started in 1936, during the heart of the Great Depression. For completeness and accuracy, Ray needed clarification on several important points regarding the early history of the business, and he hoped I could help. I was glad to be asked. This business and its schooners, past and present, have always been an important part of my life.

Ray went on: Could I verify that 1936 was, indeed, the first year? He'd found documentation of that vintage to be sparse. That was an easy one. Aside from family memory and lore, the archives in my possession had other and sufficient proof: early brochures, correspondence to and from various people, employment records, a passenger log from what was perhaps the first cruise. But Ray had a sea chest full of questions about the 25 years that my father ran the business: How did he really get the idea? When and from whom did he buy the various vessels? Where did they sail from? Could I identify this vessel and that in dozens of photographs? Did I have a photo of such and such vessels? Which schooners did my father sail as captain of, and when? The list went on and on, and grew ever longer the more he learned. It became perfectly clear that Ray loves his vessels and his business, and he wants to know *everything* about its history.

We both dug in. I'd find something of interest and inform Ray. Ray or his assistant, Margaret Jones, would find something and bring it to my attention. Fascinating stuff! At one point Ray said, "Rod, I really need to understand what was going on at the beginning of the 1939 season. Do you have any information on that?" I looked at my records and came up with a hypothesis. "Ray, I think Captain Gott must have died in the spring of 1939, probably in May or early June. Any way you can check on that?" He soon had the answer: Captain Gott had died on May 23. Another time I said that I didn't know whether so-and-so had been a cook or a mate. "Don't worry about ev-

ery crew member," Ray answered. "I just want to know how the main players were involved. You know, your father, Parker Hall, Will Shepard, Manley Grant . . . those guys." He was trying to get a handle on the big picture and the way things had been. And so it went.

The story that has emerged over the past five months, covering 75 years of operation of the same business under four different owners, is an interesting one, and is told in the pages and pictures that follow. But perhaps its most striking aspect is how little Maine Windjammer Cruises has changed in its fundamentals. Yes, the times have changed immensely, and the lives of the people who sign aboard for a cruise bear little resemblance to the lifestyles of the past—one need only look at photographs of Camden Harbor from 1940 and from today to see clear evidence of both of those changes. And, yes, the amenities provided aboard the schooners are better: electric lights instead of kerosene lanterns, lifelines to protect you from falling overboard, fewer dormitory-style cabins. But the schooners and what they offer would seem entirely familiar to time-travelers from 1940. They would come aboard, perhaps even to the same vessel that they sailed on seven decades ago. There they would find similar accommodations and friendly crews to welcome them, enjoy the same relaxing atmosphere, eat well and sumptuously—the food prepared over the same wood-burning galley stoves—make new friends among their fellow passengers and, best of all, sail the beautiful coast of Maine under a spread of sail on an old-time coaster. And that can't be beat!

In 1938, a passenger who had sailed on one of the schooners in the fleet that season wrote a newspaper article about her cruise. She closed with the prophetic words, "Long may they sail!" I am in full agreement.

Roderick Swift
Phippsburg, Maine
April 2011

Prologue

Windjammer. A simple word that conjures the romance, beauty and adventure associated with the Golden Age of Sail.

The truth is, it was originally used as a derogatory term. After thousands of years of exploration, discovery and trade that reached all corners of the globe, a new type of vessel was on the scene. It belched smoke and it didn't need the wind to propel it.

Though detested by most sailors, with improvements to reliability and efficiency steam ships were becoming increasingly popular in the latter part of the 19th Century. A natural rivalry developed between the two types of vessels competing for cargoes and livelihoods. The sailors called the steamships "stinkpots" and considered their crews less knowledgeable in the ways of the sea. The steamers considered their rivals old fashioned and said they were nothing but "windjammers," soon to become obsolete.

Well, they were right of course . . . almost. Within a few short decades the windjammers' billowing white canvas was rapidly disappearing from the horizon. Yet the sailors were proud of their heritage and of their ability to use wind as a source of power. They were proud to be called "windjammers" and they loved their way of life.

This is a story about their struggle for survival, and the story of the company whose innovation of trading cargo for passengers has kept the tradition alive.

Cargo Days

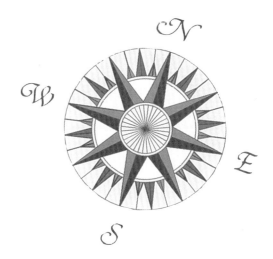

In November of 1882, Oliver Perry Smith launched a two-masted schooner in Patchogue, New York. While not extraordinary, she was an excellent model of the refined shallow-draft coasters that were common along the Eastern Seaboard. Commissioned by Smith's close friend and business associate, Edwin Bailey, this schooner would receive special care. The Bailey Lumber Mills adjacent to the shipyard provided the finest materials. The vessel's principal intended use was to bring yellow pine from Georgia and the Carolinas to meet the ever-growing demand for construction materials such as timbers, flooring and wainscoting. Edwin named his new schooner "Grace Bailey" for his daughter, born earlier that year.

The schooner's captain, Seymour Ketcham, lived aft, in the oak-paneled main cabin, which had a wood stove, table and chairs, and a few Pullman berths for the occasional guest or passenger. It was here that meals were served and the business of the vessel was conducted. On the starboard side a sliding door opened to the small but comfortable captain's sleeping quarters. Forward, the massive cargo hold stretched all the way to the foremast. Ahead, in the bow, was the fo'c'sle. Here slept a crew of four. From the helm, Captain Ketcham had easy access to his quarters in the main house as well as a commanding view of the vessel before him and her lofty rig. On deck there were three cargo hatches opening to the hold, one between the house and the mainmast, and two more between the masts. Just to port of the foremast was a small scuttle that gave access to the fo'c'sle. Aloft she carried both main and fore topmasts and topsails, as well as a flying jib set from the tip of her jibboom, 123 feet away. Grace Bailey was a powerful and handsome vessel, with a proud, hardworking crew.

While serving as a lumber carrier, Grace Bailey also made winter voyages to the West Indies in the fruit trade. After 24 years of service, in 1906 the schooner received a much-deserved rebuild. At the time, Edwin gave 1/8 share in the vessel to his favorite grandchild, Martha. As the rebuilt schooner slipped back into the water, eighteen-year-old Martha rechristened the vessel with her own nickname: "Mattie."

Steamships were now taking business from the sailing coasters, but they were not the schooners' only adversaries; railroads and trucking were connecting all of the major cities, hauling freight at an ever-increasing pace. The ports of New York, Philadelphia and Boston could no longer provide cargoes for sailing ships to many coastwise destinations. As a result, many schooners sailed Down East, to the islands and rugged coastline of Maine, which, due to its topography, had not been penetrated by rail. At the turn of the century the building and operation of sailing vessels was still viable in Maine.

No longer able to find work in her home waters, Mattie was reluctantly sold to Captain Herbert Black, of Brooksville, Maine. In November 1919 the schooner Oakwoods, owned by Captain Black, was accidently rammed and sunk by an American submarine in Buzzards Bay, near the entrance to the Cape Cod Canal. He received payment from the government for his loss, and in December 1919, Captain Black purchased the Mattie to replace her. Years later, after his death, it was discovered that the check had never been cashed. A search revealed the check hidden over a beam in the Mattie's master cabin.

Mattie served in a variety of trades, and as a general cargo carrier she hauled granite from Crotch Island to New York to help build the New York Post Office and Grand Central Station. By this time she had a yawl boat and a hoisting engine, making it possible to reduce crew size. This led to a reduction in sail area: fore topsail and flying jib were removed, and the main topsail became a light-weather sail. Alterations to the rig came about for other reasons as well: Once while getting underway, *Mattie* fell off on the wrong tack, crashing her jibboom right into a fish house, trapping the vessel. Schoonermen were not fazed by such minor incidents. Calmly, the captain went below and came up with a hand saw. He simply cut off the offending spar and sailed away. For a period she sailed with this stubby rig. No longer perfectly balanced as designed, she had a strong weather helm, requiring the mainsail to be reefed prematurely, when the breeze freshened. Eventually, the bowsprit was replaced with a longer "spike" bowsprit, eliminating the need for a jibboom.

Despite a steady decline, there was a small resurgence for sailing vessels during World War I, when anything that floated could help the cause. The Billings family of Little Deer Isle took advantage of this opportunity, building a series of five vessels, one for each Billings brother. They mostly had very businesslike names: *Enterprise, Progress, Mercantile* and *Billings Brothers*. There was one exception: *Philosopher*. All were built during the winter months, when other occupations were not available, at the Billings family homestead on the Eggemoggin Reach. To assist in the projects, a wind-powered sawmill was constructed on the site.

Launched in 1916, the *Mercantile* was the last of these Deer Isle Down Easters. Built on the beach with local materials, her construction was crude by the standards of Smith's *Grace Bailey*, but because of her graceful lines she was often referred to as "the prettiest coaster on the bay." She, too, served in a number of trades, wherever she could make a living: pulpwood from French-boro to the mills of Bucksport; firewood to the lime kilns of Rockport; fish from Swans Island to Gloucester and returning with salt, just to name a few.

Times were getting tough, and vessels couldn't support large crews. Captain Pearl Billings often sailed the *Mercantile* with just his two teenage boys. When Captain Pearl got sick he told his son Bob, only 17, to take the vessel with his brother and just follow their uncle in the *Philosopher*, which they did.

By 1930, the Depression had hit, and perhaps in some way this helped keep the windjammers going. Without the need for fuel, they could eke out a living using Mother Nature to carry them from port to port. Crew sizes continued to shrink to cut costs. However unimaginable, some famous legends of the coasting trade were known to sail alone. Captain Parker Hall was one such man, and he earned the moniker, "Lone Mariner of the New England Coast."

The typical schooner had a life expectancy of 15 to 20 years. For many, a rocky shore or a violent storm meant an early demise. For others, special care, a fortuitous rebuild or just good luck kept them going a bit longer. No matter how you sliced it, with no new coasters being built, the end of an era and a way of life was destined to come soon.

Mattie

Painting by Earle Barlow

Fully Loaded

Schooner *Mattie* with a deckload of case oil at Portland Harbor shows her working waterline. The loose-footed staysail has a short club, which was unusual and somewhat dangerous.

Photographer: John F. Leavitt
Collection: Maine Windjammer Cruises

Mercantile at Old Maid's Creek

Loaded with pulpwood headed for Bangor

Courtesy of Robert Billings
Collection: Maine Windjammer Cruises

Coaster at Monhegan

Having just left the dock under foresail, *Mattie* glides through Monhegan's narrow harbor created by Manana Island (in the background). Her taffrail runs forward to the break in the deck about midway between the masts. She is carrying a main topmast and a peapod in stern davits. Obviously without cargo, her loaded waterlines can be seen high above the surface.

Collection: Capts. Douglas K. & Linda J. Lee

Monhegan Dock

The coasting schooner *Mattie* at the public wharf of this remote island community shows her original headrig including jibboom. This artist's retreat hasn't changed much since this photo was taken nearly a century ago. Guests are fortunate to be aboard on our rare visits to this unique location.

Collection: Capts. Douglas K. & Linda J. Lee

Drying Sails

This beautiful bow shot preserved the details of *Mattie*'s head rig. Her original short staysail club has been replaced by the more common full-length spar.

Credit: E. Coffin
Collection: Maine Windjammer Cruises

Mattie awaiting Cargo

Credit: E. Coffin
Collection: Maine Windjammer Cruises

Three Lowers

Schooner *Mattie* on September 10, 1932. Her crew seem to be preoccupied by something ashore as she sails along under working canvas. The stump of her missing jibboom is still in place. Without a jib she must have had a strong weather helm in a blow. The taffrail has been cut back to the main rigging and her water barrels can be seen forward of the main house. She is also missing the starboard davit.

Photographer: R.L. Graham
Collection: Capts. Douglas K. and Linda J. Lee

Mattie

Sailing up the bay under a full load

Photographer: John F. Leavitt
Collection: Mystic Seaport Museum

Building of the Schooner Mercantile on Deer Isle

Courtesy of the Billings family
Collection: Maine Windjammer Cruises

Loading in Frenchboro

Mercantile was a familiar sight at the town wharf on Long Island. When I visited there on the *Merc* in the '80s, an old timer said he loaded plenty of pulpwood aboard her in his youth. The vessel was brought alongside at high water and was aground during most of the loading, leaving on the next tide.

Collection: Capts. Douglas K. & Linda J. Lee

Headed for the Penobscot

One of the regular cargoes for the *Mercantile* was the delivery of pulpwood to the mills of Bucksport.

Collection: Capts. Douglas K. & Linda J. Lee

Upriver

The *Mercantile* sails in company with another lumber schooner up the Penobscot.

Collection: Capts. Douglas K. & Linda J. Lee

Lovely Mabel

Schooner *Mabel* loading lumber from a temporary wharf at Indian Rest, New Meadows River, Maine

Collection: Capts. Douglas K. & Linda J. Lee

A Passion-Born Idea

In 1930, 28-year-old Frank Swift, from Poughkeepsie, New York, was coming to Maine for summers. Having been enthralled as a child by stories about his great uncle, who went to sea as a harpooner aboard a whaling ship, Frank enrolled in King's Point Merchant Marine Academy and served as a cadet aboard the New York State sail/motor training vessel *Newport*. By age 20, he was a quartermaster aboard a Barber line steamship sailing for the Orient carrying case oil. He soon realized that life aboard a steamer was not going to satisfy his passion for the sea and sailing ships, so he left that service to pursue a career as an artist. This eventually led him to Maine, where he worked as a set designer and director for Camp Wigwam, in South Waterford, and later at Camp Blue Moon, on Toddy Pond, in East Orland.

Frank enjoyed watching the pulpwood schooners unloading in nearby Bucksport, and went aboard a few to ask if he could charter a boat to bring his campers sailing. Eventually, he met Captain Parker Hall, who agreed to take them on his schooner *George Gress*. With straw in the holds for bedding and a curtain down the middle to separate the boys from the girls, they were off for a week's adventure. This cruise, which became an annual event, was the highlight of the summer for everyone at the camp, but especially for Frank, who was being drawn closer to his true calling.

In 1935, Frank relocated permanently to Maine, building a cabin on Toddy Pond near the camp. That first winter he made jewelry to survive. During those long winter nights he dreamt of sailing down the bay with a free wind and a lovely coasting schooner underfoot. But Frank was a realist, and the reality was he needed to find a way to support his young family. He knew it was a hard chance to make a living as a coasterman.

His memories of sailing aboard the *Gress* with Captain Hall were so enjoyable, he thought that others might be willing to pay for the experience. What if he got a schooner and instead of hauling freight, carried people on cruises along the Maine coast?

Frank sought the advice of Captain Hall, who suggested he talk with Otis Shepard, owner of the trim little schooner *Mabel*, which was idle. Captain Otis wanted to sell her, but he agreed to charter *Mabel* to Frank so he could try out his idea for one year. Otis, probably thinking the plan was foolish, insisted that Frank would have to remove any accommodations he built for his guests before returning the vessel.

Frank bought lumber on credit to make the necessary modifications. Rough house structures were built above each cargo hatch. He simply covered their tops in canvas, tacked down to keep out the weather. He then divided the holds, boarding them off into comfortable cabins, each with two built-in bunks and a small hatch to access the deck. Otis' brother, Captain Will Shepard, of Deer Isle, agreed to go as skipper, with his wife as cook. Swift then approached several travel agencies about booking passengers, but they would have nothing to do with it. These were not cruise liners or even proper yachts. "Who'd pay to sail aboard an old cargo boat, sleep in a converted cargo hold, and work on the ship besides?" Frank was of a different mind. True, accommodations were spartan, but the food would be good and the guests didn't really have to work unless they wanted to. Besides, what he was really selling was adventure.

Undeterred, he placed a few tiny advertisements in city newspapers, offering "Vacations Under Sail." That summer he sailed from Jose Hobbs' lumber wharf, on Camden's Bay View Street.

The protected inner harbor offered all of the services Frank would need and the port was perfectly situated for embarking on cruises exploring the beautiful islands and bays of mid-coast Maine.

The town itself was lovely, a quiet little New England seaport that had already become a destination for summer visitors. With the Camden Hills as a backdrop and waterfalls cascading into the tidewater, it had a reputation as the prettiest harbor in Maine. As beautiful as the harbor was, Camden's hardworking waterfront was still a bit rough around the edges. Swift's first potential customers were two genteel ladies who had themselves chauffeured up from Boston. When they reached Hobbs' busy lumberyard they looked down the steep ladder in disdain at the rough-sided schooner, with its cargo-scarred decks, and left.

Swift's first actual passengers were also ladies from Boston, three adventuresome schoolteachers who arrived in Camden filled with enthusiasm. By morning, they were shipmates, flying east'rd under a cloud of canvas, learning the life of the old days of sail. The next week Swift had no passengers at all, but they sailed anyway. So it went; that first season, the most *Mabel* carried on a single cruise was five passengers.

Every week was a new adventure, not only for the passengers but for Frank as well. They visited many of the ports frequented by the coasters, such as the bustling fishing and quarry town of Stonington, on Deer Isle, or the out-of-the-way lumber port of Frenchboro, Long Island. Other days were spent strolling about quaint coastal villages or exploring uninhabited islands.

Mrs. Shepard kept them all well fed with roasts, chowders and plenty of fresh baked goods from the wood cookstove, and all were welcomed in her warm, comfortable galley. She also prepared the abundant supply of fish caught by the guests anytime they wanted seafood on the menu. Throughout the summer, Frank and Captain Will provided them with thrilling sailing as they navigated well-traveled waterways, like the Fox Islands Thorofare and Merchants Row. They sailed across vast interconnecting bays and weaved through hundreds of peaceful, spruce-clad islands. Some trips took them offshore, where they saw whales, on their way to more remote islands like Matinicus and Monhegan.

By the end of the summer Frank felt his guests were provided with a very special experience. Even though he had a loss of $210, Frank was convinced he was on to something, and knew he had to try again the following year.

Captain Frank Swift
Courtesy of Rod Swift

Mabel, 1936
Courtesy of Rod Swift

Mabel from Astern
Courtesy of Rod Swift

Aboard the Mabel
Courtesy of Rod Swift

Taking Hold

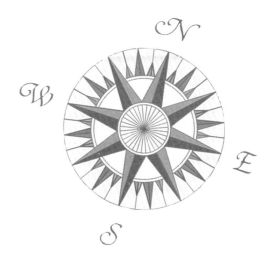

As agreed, Swift returned the *Mabel* to Otis Shepard, who sold her to a sardine cannery Down East, and Captain Will returned to the coasting trade, buying the *Mattie* from Herbert Black. Meanwhile, Frank chartered another idle schooner, the *Lydia M. Webster* out of Belfast, and began preparing for his second season. Her owner, a colorful old seafarer named Ralph Randall Gott, loved a good time and was happy to be captain aboard Frank's cruises. Cap had spent his life on what he liked to call "the Belfast Ocean." He knew the waters like the back of his hand, but was handicapped by short sightedness. He always stayed within sight of land and when the fog rolled in he would find a place to lower anchor and "set a spell." Frank, who was learning the ways of the coastermen, would prove to be a valuable assistant.

Passengers who had sailed the previous year were returning, and telling their friends as well. Word of mouth was responsible for most of Frank's business. Still, that second year Frank was only modestly successful, doing slightly better than breaking even. He was starting to get discouraged about his prospects with the business but decided to give it one more year. Late in the season, he got a break when Gwendoline Keene, a sailing enthusiast and travel writer, heard about his cruises. She wrote a page-two article for the Sunday *Boston Herald* featuring a picture of salty Captain Gott at the wheel of the "*Liddy*" and a very complimentary story about Frank's cruises, saying, "these ships are gateways to pure enchantment." This was just the spark he needed to get the attention of city folk looking for a change of pace.

The *Webster* often sailed in company, or shared a harbor with the other cargo-carrying schooners. Frank and his cruises were becoming known to the coastermen. While the old timers at first considered these tourist trips an oddity, they eventually admired Frank's ingenuity in finding a cargo that loaded itself! Frank was becoming one of them.

Believing his idea was sound, Frank committed himself and began looking to buy a vessel of his own. The *Annie F. Kimball* had retired, and Frank could have her cheap. He asked Captain Manley Grant to accompany him to look her over. When they arrived at Great Wass Island they found her run up on the beach in need of much repair. Captain Grant said she had possibilities, so Frank bought her for $700. They spent several days caulking the vessel, then sailed her to Sandy Point where they grounded her out for further repairs. Here carpenters, painters and riggers grateful to have work prepared her for cruising in short order.

Frank returned to Camden with a fleet for his third season. Captain Gott continued in the *Lydia M. Webster* and Frank took command of his own schooner, *Annie F. Kimball*. Captain Grant went along for the first few trips to assist aboard the new schooner. Thanks to Gwendoline's article, working-class people were reading how they could now enjoy a sailing vacation on the beautiful coast of Maine, an exclusive privilege previously available to only the wealthiest yachtsmen. Things were starting to pick up. Later that summer, Gwendoline sailed with Captain Frank aboard the *Annie F. Kimball*, and people were about to read a lot more.

As on any sea voyage, passengers were often moved to draw or keep a log in an effort to capture the beauty of this experience. On August 23, 1938, in one such log, Elizabeth Carmer wrote: "In the morning I lay in my bed listening to the screaming of the seagulls and the soft lap, lap of the water on the side of the vessel until Pierre (the cook) rapped on each hatch shouting 'Rise and shine!' The scents of pine and wild roses, blown out from the land, joined the smells of the sea, of the tar and hemp, and of coffee boiling on the stove in the galley. On the deck we filled granite basins from a water barrel and, noting the direction of the wind, washed our faces at the rail. The second day had started on the *Annie F. Kimball*."

In a later entry she wrote: "Long after the music had ended we sat and watched the aurora borealis. Great shafts of light shot up from the horizon, met and quivered in vibrating waves in the center of the sky. And as we watched a blazing meteor streaked across the sky." Yes, there was something very special and unique about these new Windjammer Cruises, and many thousands found out about it when Elizabeth's journal appeared in *Harper's Bazaar*.

For schoonermen and their families, sailing this rugged coast was a way of life passed down for centuries. Though not as luxurious as yachting, there was a reality to this experience that was the essence of what Swift was offering. Little did he know that his tenacity for preserving this way of life would be responsible for saving so many vessels or giving distant generations the opportunity to relive the "Golden Days of Sail."

In 1939, encouraged by the relative success of the previous season and his advanced bookings, Frank contacted Will Shepard to charter his schooner *Mattie* for the months of July and August. Captain Will must have found his earlier experiences cruising aboard the *Mabel* more enjoyable than the rough life of a coasterman, since he agreed, and returned to serve as *Mattie*'s captain. *Mattie*, far larger, would carry more passengers than the *Webster* and the *Kimball* combined. It was Frank's plan to operate these three schooners during what he expected to be a banner year, but shortly before sailing, on May 23, Captain Gott died. Uncertain about the future of the vessel, Swift again turned to his friend Manley Grant. The captain helped Frank find another schooner, *Clinton*, which he purchased on June 15. Manley offered to go as captain, and with his assistance Frank's new schooner was ready to sail by July 3.

During that spring and summer, stories about Gwendoline's 1938 cruise with Frank appeared in no fewer than seven metropolitan newspapers, including the *New York Times*, *Boston Herald* and the *Christian Science Monitor*. With this and Elizabeth's article (published that winter), Swift's three ships were filled to capacity and he had to turn many away!

Gott's widow eventually sold the *Webster* to Connie Grant, Manley's brother, who was a close family friend. Connie then approached Frank with an offer to sell him the *Lydia M. Webster* for his cruises if he could remain aboard as captain. A deal was struck and the *Webster* returned to the fleet in 1940. That year Frank also purchased the *Mattie* from Will Shepard, who would retire at the end of the season. Things were going so well that Frank bought a third vessel, the *Lois M. Candage*, in mid-summer. She arrived with a large wheelhouse, which needed to be removed prior to putting her into service with his fleet near the end of that season.

By now this phenomenon had caught the eye of America. That summer, Frank's vacations appeared on the cover of *Life* Magazine, and there were feature articles in *Cue* and in *Reader's Digest*. Captain Swift now owned and operated a fleet of five schooners; the Great Depression was over and there seemed to be ever-growing demand for his Windjammer Cruises. Frank Swift's dream was a reality, his business was a success, and Camden had become known as the "Windjammer Capital of the World."

Lydia M. Webster
Entering Camden Harbor
Collection: Capts. Douglas K. & Linda J. Lee

Lydia M. Webster
On the beach at Sandy Point
Photographer: Montgomery

Annie F. Kimball & Lydia M. Webster
At Hobbs Wharf, Camden Harbor
Courtesy of Rod Swift

Passengers
A trip aboard the *Webster*, 1937
Courtesy of Rod Swift

Lobster Dinner
Fresh from the boat, 1937
Courtesy of Rod Swift

Winter at Sandy Point
Lydia M. Webster, Clinton, Annie F. Kimball and *George Gress*
Collection: Capts. Douglas K. & Linda J. Lee

Winter Storage
Capt. Parker Hall would watch Swift's fleet during the winter months.
Collection: Capts. Douglas K. & Linda J. Lee

Mattie
Southwest Harbor, 1940
Collection: Capts. Douglas K. & Linda J. Lee

Mattie
Courtesy of Rod Swift

Clinton and Lois M. Candage
Candage joined the fleet with a distinctive large wheelhouse.
Collection: Capts. Douglas K. & Linda J. Lee

Lois M. Candage
Courtesy of Maine Windjammer Cruises
Collection: Bex

Annie F. Kimball and Lois M. Candage
Courtesy of Rod Swift

July 1940 trip on the Mattie from the scrapbook of passenger Ruth E. Eddy
Courtesy of Carol Bortell Hess

Winner of the *New York Herald Tribune* photo contest. Taken by Ruth E. Eddy on her trip aboard the *Mattie*.
Courtesy of Carol Bortell Hess

Windjammer Cruises, 1939
Schooners *Kimball, Mattie, Webster* and *Clinton*
Courtesy of Rod Swift

Smooth Sailing

In 1941, Frank's fleet of windjammers sailed each Monday morning from June to September. A crowd of onlookers, both visitors and locals alike, often appeared at the docks to watch the vessels getting underway. One-week trips were offered for $38, and two-week vacations for only $70. Since destinations always varied from week to week, there was seldom duplication, and many guests booked consecutive trips, enjoying a brief stopover in Camden Harbor (to which the schooners returned each Saturday afternoon). Passengers cared for their own cabins and usually brought their own blankets, which were often sent ahead by express or parcel post.

The lure of the sea and the romance of a tall ship had wide appeal to tourists who flocked from across the country for Frank's carefree, unscheduled adventures. Amateur sailors and land lubbers alike were invited to haul at halyard and sheet, stand a trick at the wheel or just laze in the salt air and sunshine, feeling the ship, alive and scudding along under full sail. Frank was an artist and with his passion for the experience he painted a picture with words of this life under sail. He described sparkling summer days on the heeling deck of a Yankee schooner and placid starlit nights swinging at anchor in snug Down East harbors. The cruises were always more than expected and the passengers, who were never disappointed, continued to come back for more.

All of the old timers who sailed Swift's windjammers were veterans of many years in the coasting trade. For the passengers, getting to know them was part of the fun. Totally at ease in their environment, each of the captains could show even the most experienced a thing or two about sailing, and they had a lifetime of sea stories to keep the guests entertained.

Frank took command of his newest addition, the *Lois M. Candage*. Captains Manley and Connie continued in the *Clinton* and the *Webster*. Captain Will Shepard had retired and Frank needed a skipper for the big schooner *Mattie*. He knew just the man for the job. Captain Parker Hall had been a close friend and mentor to Frank since those first days sailing with the campers aboard the *George Gress*. During the winters he would keep an eye on Swift's schooners, along with the *Gress*, near his home in Stockton Springs. He was a giant of a man who had a personality and a reputation to match. Having admired the fine sailing qualities of the *Mattie* for years, Parker was pleased to accept Frank's offer to sail the vessel.

After two years aboard the *Mattie*, Parker heard that Zeb Tilton, another legendary coasterman, was selling his famous schooner *Alice Wentworth*. This was the only vessel of her class that was considered a match for the *Mattie* and Parker felt he must have her. The two captains had much in common.

When Captain Hall arrived in Martha's Vineyard to buy the *Wentworth*, 75-year-old Zeb said he had one small load that still needed to be delivered to the mainland, and invited Hall to come along. The two captains made the delivery and soon returned to the island. Zeb went ashore, leaving Parker aboard his new schooner. A friend of Zeb's from the island stopped by to welcome him home but met only the new captain. In an effort to make conversation he asked, "How was your trip to the mainland?" Parker replied, "The trip was fine, but that old man [referring to Zeb] doesn't know a thing about sailing." The islander caught up with Zeb later in town. Curious, he asked, "How was your trip to the mainland?" Zeb responded, "The trip was fine, but that Captain Hall, he can't sail worth a darn." The next day, 82-year-old Parker Hall left for Gloucester, alone!

Lydia M. Webster
Under sail
Courtesy of Rod Swift

Wing and Wing
Mattie, Clinton and *Kimball* sailing wing and wing.
Courtesy of Rod Swift

Annie F. Kimball
Courtesy of Rod Swift

Clinton
Courtesy of Rod Swift

Early Captains
Capts. Parker Hall, Manley Grant, Frank Swift and Ralph Randall Gott

Hall, Grant & Swift - Courtesy of Rod Swift
Gott - Collection: Capts. Douglas K. & Linda J. Lee

Holding Course

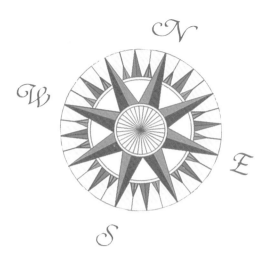

With the US entry into World War II, Frank hoped he could somehow help the effort. He offered his vessels for war service and the *Mattie* became the first training vessel for the Maine Maritime Academy. Having considerable experience, Frank made application for a commission in the Navy Reserves, but due to colorblindness his application was denied. During the war years, cruises continued but they were somewhat restricted and never went offshore. There was an austerity aboard, but there was also the serenity that the peaceful waters of Penobscot Bay offered to the guests during this troubled time. Most of the passengers were single women, and some cabins were converted to dormitory-style quarters with four or five bunks. Occasionally the ship's roster would include a soldier on furlough.

In 1942, Frank purchased two more vessels. The large schooner yacht *Indra*, which technically was part of the fleet but was advertised separately from the coasters, offered a slightly more upscale sailing experience. The second vessel was the *Hattie Loring*, a coaster that had an auxiliary engine installed. Swift never used her for passengers. Instead he continued to operate her carrying cargo to and from the islands of Penobscot and Blue Hill bays, while basing out of Camden.

In 1943, Frank bought two properties on the Camden waterfront, extending from Bay View Street down to the harbor adjacent to the town landing. With seven vessels he continued to lease dock space throughout the harbor, but this gave him a base of operations from which to work and it included a slipway that he used regularly for minor repairs. Frank's business had become a considerable factor in the local economy. He employed captains, crews, repairmen and office staff.

He kept grocers and other suppliers busy, and Camden merchants did a brisk business selling rain slickers, wide-brimmed sun hats and other items to the steady stream of visitors who came to sail the schooners.

Sadly that year, *Annie F. Kimball* proved too weak for service, and she again was run up on the flats, this time never returning to sea, her bones laid to rest behind a granite wall on the far side of Camden Harbor. That same year Frank purchased the *Enterprise*, one of the Billings' vessels. For a short while she was part of his cargo fleet along with the *Hattie Loring*. More adventuresome passengers were welcome aboard for the experience, but she soon replaced the *Kimball* as a cruise schooner, with Swift at the helm.

In 1944, Frank retired the *Lydia M. Webster* after eight years of cruising service. Her condition would require repairs too costly to justify, so she was stripped of her gear and scuttled off Mark Island, in deep water. *Webster* was replaced that season by the schooner *Lillian*, maintaining a fleet of six cruise vessels, plus the *Hattie Loring*. Up to that time there was no shortage of retired schooners that still had life in them. They could be bought cheap and converted quickly. That situation was about to change.

Enterprise and Mercantile

Drawing a crowd at Swift's wharf

Courtesy of Rod Swift

Enterprise

Collection: Capts. Douglas K. & Linda J. Lee

Enterprise

Spring overhaul at Camden Shipyard, *Mattie* across the harbor at Hobbs Lumber Wharf

Courtesy of Maine Windjammer Cruises

Collection: Bex

Lillian

Courtesy of Rod Swift

Swift's Camden Harbor Property

A view of Swift's dock and the slipway from Camden Harbor

Courtesy of Maine Windjammer Cruises

Collection: Bex

Clinton

In the slipway

Photographer: Carroll Thayer Berry

Courtesy of Penobscot Marine Museum

Swift's Wharf

Drying sails

Courtesy of Rod Swift

All Aboard with Captain Swift

With the end of the war, good times were back in full swing. More and more people were coming to enjoy the cruises and business was booming. Frank bought two more vessels: *Eva S. Cullison* and *Mercantile*; the latter was another Billings schooner and sister ship to the *Enterprise*. He considered the *Cullison* a fine vessel and chose to sail her for the next eight years. He now had a fleet of nine schooners, with eight offering Windjammer Cruises and one still in the cargo trade.

There was a continued fascination with this unusual vacation option, and travel writers never seemed to tire of stories about Frank's adventures. The more they read, the more they came, people from all walks of life and from across the country. It didn't matter that the amenities were few, in fact that was part of the charm. There was no segregation of first class and steerage. In fact all were equal as they pulled on a line or sat shoulder to shoulder around a common table sharing a meal. Shopkeepers, office workers, doctors, farmers, even congressmen and movie stars could be found among the ships' compliment. They all shared one thing in common, the love of the sea and a sailing ship.

Competitors began offering similar cruises. An in-depth article in *Liberty* Magazine in 1945 about Swift's windjammers stated, "As proof of the success of his cruises, other operators confess frankly that they are copying his methods." Nearby Rockland had a schooner sailing all summer, and there were others in Chesapeake Bay and Long Island Sound as well.

By 1946, Frank was out of the cargo business. Retiring the *Hattie Loring*, he dismantled her and used her parts to keep his other vessels going. After 10 years, he was happy to bring the *Mabel* back into the fleet. The sturdy little vessel that had launched his business in 1936 was up for sale

by the sardine factory. Frank purchased her and brought her back to Camden. *Mabel*'s rig had been removed and she had been registered as having gas screw propulsion. Over the next few years she would be rerigged and have her engine removed, becoming a windjammer once again.

In 1947, eleven years after Frank Swift founded Windjammer Cruises, a man by the name of Mike Schwartz started a sailing business with a small sloop out of Florida. He eventually purchased larger, foreign-flagged vessels that could not pass US Coast Guard regulation, and he moved the company offshore. The vessels were held in a series of foreign registries and stayed clear of US waters. Operating in the generally unregulated Caribbean, Schwartz, a self-proclaimed pirate, changed his name to Burke and began advertising as "Windjammer Cruises." This created considerable confusion. Eventually he agreed to change the name of his business to "Windjammer Barefoot Cruises," and Frank's fleet eventually became known as "Maine Windjammer Cruises."

Captain Swift owned a total of 10 vessels when the former pilot schooner *Yankee* joined the fleet in 1948. With a price of $10,000, she was by far the most expensive vessel Frank had ever bought. She had been owned by Irving Johnson, who had made several circumnavigations (with paying crewmembers to support the effort). Frank intended to offer a more luxurious sailing experience and he hired extra crew, expecting passengers just to sit back and enjoy the ride. Thinking they were missing out on the fun, passengers joined in anyway. *Yankee* only served one season in Swift's fleet. With her deep draft, she was more suited to offshore work and Frank wanted to try another idea.

In 1949, Frank attempted to diversify by offering cruises in other areas. He went into partnership with Walter Boudreau, and they took *Yankee* to Nova Scotia, offering similar trips in those waters. But Frank eventually withdrew from this enterprise, and *Yankee* was lost when she sank in the Bras d'Or Lake. That same year Frank went into partnership with Captain Jim Nisbet, selling an interest in the schooner *Mabel* and forming a company called "Vacations Under Sail," which operated the vessel out of South Freeport, Maine. These were the first steps in the reduction of Camden's windjammer fleet.

Maine Coast Schooner Cruise

Old Yankee schooners carry 'dry land sailors' on cruises in coastal waters

Old-time Yankee schooners are sailing again in Maine's coastal waters. But today, they carry a new kind of cargo. Throughout the summer, fleets of the two-masters sail from fishing villages with capacity loads of "dry land sailors."

At Camden, located on Penobscot Bay, Captain Frank Swift's Windjammer Fleet takes vacationists on week-long cruises to islands in the Bay, and to historic villages along the coast.

Sailing with the tides and wind, the schooners anchor in different harbors every night. Highlights of the week are lobster dinners on deck, old-fashioned country dances, beach parties and visits to old landmarks ashore.

Although listed as passengers, most of the landlubbers serve as able-bodied seamen. They swab decks, help tend sails, learn to read charts and steer the vessels. Most discover a new weakness for old two-masters.

Seafaring vacationists bask in afternoon sunshine on deck of the schooner *Enterprise* as she cruises among spruce-covered islands in Maine's Penobscot Bay.

Sailing out of Camden's harbor, the *Enterprise* passes another old, two-masted schooner, *Maggie*, also carrying a party of vacationing landlubbers.

Fresh boiled lobster dinner on deck is customary Friday dinner during cruises. Mate shows vacationists how to open a lobster without tools.

Mate Gregory Merchant, a veteran sailing vessel hand, plays his mandolin and sings sea ballads. Guests often bring instruments, play at dances.

Cruisers spend leisurely hours on the six-day trip playing rummy on the deck. In the evening, they went ashore for beach parties and dances.

With the 'Enterprise' at anchor, three members of the cruise go over the side for an early morning swim. But chilly air discouraged most others.

Landlubbers bear a hand with schooner's rigging. They also "stood a trick" at the wheel, learned to read charts, set and take in the sails.

MAINE COAST SCHOONER CRUISE *continued*

Early risers help swab the decks on a crisp morning, while other landlubbers pump bilges. After their chore, girls begged warm water for cold feet.

Line on boat davit serves as a clothesline for swimmers' wet bathing suits. In background is an island in Bay where the schooner anchored.

In small cabins accommodating three persons, these girls found schooner's slight roll restful. None of cruisers got seasick in the calm waters.

Windjammer Dance at Stonington attracts cruisers from most schooners in Camden fleet. Old-timers of area often join in dancing the reels.

Ashore in Camden, vacationists visit curio shops, landmarks. Flower boxes on lamp posts are gifts to town from wife of musician Efrem Zimbalist.

At a sardine cannery on Mount Desert Island, the seafarers watch great baskets of sardines waiting to be processed. Cannery packs 60,000 cases a year.

The six-day cruise ended, these "old salts" view Camden's quiet harbor, which opens into Penobscot Bay. In recent years, the little lobster-fishing town has become one of Maine's most popular vacation centers. It attracts not only sailing enthusiasts, but many leading musicians and artists.

Tips for Maine Coast Visitors

1. Leaving Boston, travelers can drive the length of the Maine coast to the Canadian border on U.S. Highway 1. Special summer trains and buses from New York and Boston run to important harbor towns.

2. Schooner cruises from Camden and Rockland usually begin on Mondays, last six days. Reservations may be made for two-week cruise.

3. For cruises with the Windjammer Fleet, which operates out of Camden, passengers are required to furnish own bedding, linen. The fare is $45 per week—not including Federal tax —for meals, cabin, and entertainment.

4. Write State of Maine Publicity Bureau, 3 St. John St., Portland, Me., for detailed vacation information.

For vacation bulletins, send stamped, addressed envelope to LOOK *Magazine, 511 Fifth Avenue, New York, N. Y.*

After the cruise, the 'Enterprise' takes a rest, moors between sister schooners

MAINE
Belfast
Castine
Lincolnville
Mt. Desert
Camden
Stonington
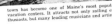

Webster, Clinton and *Candage*
At Hobbs Lumber Wharf
Courtesy of Maine Windjammer Cruises
Collection: Bex

Eva S. Cullison
Courtesy of John Jackson

Cullison
Making the turn at the head of the harbor to come alongside the *Enterprise*
Courtesy of Maine Windjammer Cruises

Mattie and Enterprise
Captains Grant and Cotton on deck, Kip Grant on the float
Courtesy of Rod Swift

Swift's Fleet at Anchor
Lillian, Enterprise, Candage, and *Mattie*
Courtesy of Rod Swift

Winter in Camden Harbor
Cullison, Enterprise, Mercantile, Mattie, Candage
Courtesy of Rod Swift

Mattie Leaving Dock in Camden
Courtesy of Rod Swift

Magazine Articles, 1940s
Early magazine articles captured the imagination of readers across the country.
Courtesy of Rod Swift

Look Magazine, July 8, 1947
Courtesy of Rod Swift

Camden Harbor
Collection: Capts. Douglas K. & Linda J. Lee

Yankee
Courtesy of Rod Swift

Mattie, Indra and Cullison
Photograph: Winifred Walker
Courtesy of Rod Swift

Shorten Sail

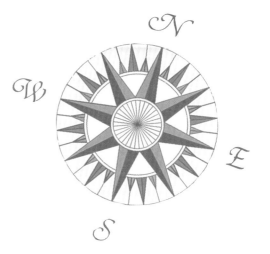

As part of his restructuring, Frank also took *Lillian* out of the fleet that year. She went under the command of Captain Converse Grant for several seasons, offering day sails out of Belfast. In the spring of 1955, when she was just "plum worn out," Captain Grant ran her up on a mud bank on the Penobscot River, near his home at Sandy Point.

By the middle of the 20th Century the tide had turned. Finding old coasters that were suitable for service was a thing of the past. Frank's aging fleet had ever-increasing demands for repairs, and it was becoming difficult to find captains as well. The fleet began to shrink. In the fall of 1951, when the boats were laid up in Camden, *Indra* had the inside berth. A late-season hurricane with huge waves caused the outboard vessel to crush the lighter-built schooner yacht. Damage was beyond repair, and she was salvaged for parts, including her 14-ton lead keel.

Frank had a business model that said never spend more to maintain a vessel than it cost to buy her. He did this for many years, but by now most of his veteran cargo ships had served for more than half a century, and this philosophy would have to be rethought. When the big schooner *Mattie* needed repairs in 1952, Swift undertook an extensive and expensive rebuild. She was the finest schooner in the fleet and he could not let her go. To help finance the repairs, Frank sold the *Clinton* to Dick Parshall, who operated her out of Castine. Only a few seasons later, when she went to the shipyard for spring haul out, they found her too rotten to continue. She spent the rest of her days there in Stonington.

Meanwhile it appeared the waters of southern Maine did not have as much to offer as beautiful Penobscot Bay, and in 1952 the *Mabel* returned to Camden. Vacations Under Sail was dissolved and the vessel sold back to Swift's original fleet. This was the same year that the *Eva S. Cullison* carried her last passengers. She remained at the dock for several years while Frank tried to find a suitable home for her. Mystic Seaport agreed to accept her, but could not raise the funds to restore and maintain the schooner, so Frank gave her to the Sea Scouts in Rockland. Eventually, they sold her to an amusement park in Rockport, Massachusetts, where she spent her final days as a tourist attraction.

During the '50s, a passenger schooner broke up when caught in a hurricane while operating in Chesapeake Bay, causing considerable loss of life. As a result, the Coast Guard started rigorous inspections of similar vessels. Some say too rigorous, but in any event the severity of the circumstances caused everyone to take a more conservative approach. It was determined that vessels carrying paying passengers would be held to a higher standard of scrutiny, accelerating their removal from service.

When Frank retired *Mabel* in 1954, she too remained at the dock. Eventually he sold her to Harvey Kelley, a school teacher who also worked summers as a captain. Kelley lived aboard *Mabel* for two winters and a summer with his family, including his daughter, Margaret, who now works for Maine Windjammer Cruises. Those years living and sailing aboard *Mabel* are among her finest childhood memories. Kelley sold *Mabel* to two young men from Boston. Against his advice, the new owners set out to return home during a gale. The vessel was lost, and the crew was rescued by the Coast Guard.

When the *Cullison* retired, Frank returned to the *Lois M. Candage*, which he sailed for the next four years until she, too, succumbed to old age. After her last season, 1956, she also ended up as a tourist attraction, this time at the Saltwater Farm Pier Restaurant in Damariscotta, where she finally settled into the mud. Frank then took command of the *Mattie*. *Enterprise* was the last vessel to retire from his fleet. In 1957, after being stripped of her gear at the Camden Shipyard, *Enterprise* was towed to a beach in Camden's outer harbor, where she was burned.

By this time, Frank's fleet had been reduced to just two vessels but they were his two largest. The *Mattie* was now 75 years old (and had undergone her considerable rebuild), and *Mercantile* was relatively young at only 51. During his final four years in the business, Frank sailed *Mattie* as his flagship. He never thought he would enjoy sailing a big schooner, but he was surprised how comfortable and handy she was in spite of her size.

In all Captain Swift operated a total of 13 vessels during his 25-year career in the windjammer trade—an industry he created—in the tiny New England seaport of Camden, Maine. The proud *Mattie* and *Mercantile* carried on with their clipper bows and hempen rigging, giving vacationers a thrill under sail aboard true merchant ships. The word "windjammer" had a new meaning, and these relics from a past era had a new purpose. Because of him, they would live on, to give many adventuresome travelers a glimpse of the Golden Age of Sail.

Mattie
Courtesy of Maine Windjammer Cruises
Collection: Bex

Drying Sails in Camden Harbor
Mabel, Clinton, Enterprise, Mattie and Mercantile
Courtesy of Penobscot Marine Museum

Schooners Drying Sails
Courtesy of Maine Windjammer Cruises
Collection: Bex

Camden Harbor
Courtesy of Maine Windjammer Cruises
Collection: Bex

Swift's Wharf
Courtesy of Rod Swift

Candage
A visit to Buck Harbor
Courtesy of Rod Swift

Mabel
Photographer: Carroll Thayer Berry
Courtesy of Rod Swift

Mabel
Courtesy of Rod Swift

Candage
Passing Curtis Island Light
Courtesy of Rod Swift

Mattie
Under sail in the early 1950s
Courtesy of Maine Windjammer Cruises
Collection: Bex

Mercantile
Under sail in the early 1950s
Courtesy of Maine Windjammer Cruises
Collection: Bex

Enterprise Passenger Scrapbook, 1955
Grace Black Wood and fellow passengers, including then-crewmember Rod Swift
Photographs: Grace Black Wood
Collection: Maine Windjammer Cruises

Candage Passenger Scrapbook, 1955
Passengers sailing with Frank Swift aboard the *Candage*
Collection: Maine Windjammer Cruises

Mattie
Photograph: Wide World Photos
Collection: Capts. Douglas K. & Linda J. Lee

Last Days of the Enterprise
Courtesy of Penobscot Marine Museum and Maine Windjammer Cruises
Collection: Bex

Mattie
Courtesy of Maine Windjammer Cruises
Collection: Bex

Mercantile
Collection: Capts. Douglas K. & Linda J. Lee

Mattie and Mercantile
September 1959
Courtesy of Maine Windjammer Cruises
Collection: Bex

Mercantile and Mattie
Photograph: Carroll Thayer Berry
Courtesy of Maine Windjammer Cruises
Collection: Bex

Carry On

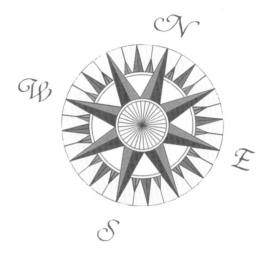

In 1961, Frank sold Maine Windjammer Cruises to his former partner in Vacations Under Sail, Captain Jim Nisbet, who continued operations with the *Mattie* and *Mercantile* through the '60s. For several years he watched a small vessel being constructed on Deer Island. When he stopped one day to check on progress, the owner said he was losing interest. Jim thought she would make a fine little schooner and bought her for his business. She was brought to the Camden Shipyard, where she was fitted out as a smaller version of her big sisters, *Mattie* and *Merc*. While discussing possible names for the schooner one of the crew said, "The only thing that would be worth all the money you have spent is a mistress," and that was her name: *Mistress*.

Jim also owned another business, Vagabond Shanty Cruises, which offered sightseeing trips on a river barge in Florida. He didn't purchase the wharf from Swift, and eventually moved the schooners to their current berth in the center of the harbor. During the winter he would bring them to Billings' shipyard in Stonington to be looked after, and then he would bring them back to Camden after spring haul out.

Captain Nisbet operated the fleet for less than a decade. Les and Ann Bex had fallen in love with Camden and the schooners when they'd made a cruise a few years earlier. In subsequent years Les, an engineer, managed to get a few weeks off each summer and spent them as a deckhand aboard the schooners. He and Ann bought the business in 1969. Their first season, Les was again a deckhand, aboard the *Mercantile*. After the season he wanted to work on repairs himself, so he kept the boats in Camden during the winter. That first year, while work was being done near their berth, Les brought the schooners to a dock by the old lumber wharf that Swift first sailed from. This was a bit exposed for winter use, and the vessels were almost lost in a huge storm.

During the 1970 season, Les decided to stay ashore and just manage the business. That August, in an unfortunate accident, the *Mattie* went aground on a ledge near Stonington. Camden's harbormaster brought Les to the boat, and they put a temporary patch on her. On the next tide the vessel was towed to the shipyard where they work tirelessly for 10 days. The *Mattie* returned to Camden, where she was greeted with cannon salutes, sounding of horns, and cheers from all the well wishers. Les finished out the season serving as captain himself.

For several years thereafter Les sailed as captain aboard the *Mercantile*. He spent his winters making repairs and improvements to the schooners. With the ever-increasing pace of more modern times, the importance of preserving these vessels—and the experience they afforded—grew with each year. The *Mercantile* was approaching 70, and the *Mattie* was almost 100 years old. It was all he could do to stay ahead of the work required to keep them afloat. Yet he managed to do so for 17 years.

Captain Jim Nesbit
Courtesy of Maine Windjammer Cruises
Collection: Bex

Captain Les Bex
Caulking the *Mercantile*
Courtesy of Maine Windjammer Cruises
Collection: Bex

Drying Sails
Courtesy of Rod Swift

Mattie and Mecantile
Courtesy of Maine Windjammer Cruises
Collection: Bex

Schooner Mistress
Courtesy of Maine Windjammer Cruises
Collection: Bex

Mattie
Stern view
Courtesy of Maine Windjammer Cruises
Collection: Bex

Mercantile Passenger Images, 1977
Images from "Old Salts" Ed and Barbara Wandersee's third *Mercantile* cruise
Photograph: Wandersee
Collection: Maine Windjammer Cruises

Winter Storm
Courtesy of Maine Windjammer Cruises
Collection: Bex

Run Aground
Courtesy of Maine Windjammer Cruises
Collection: Bex

Camden Harbor
Courtesy of Maine Windjammer Cruises
Collection: Bex

Three Windjammers
Mistress, Mercantile and *Grace Bailey*
Courtesy of Maine Windjammer Cruises
Collection: Bex

My Watch

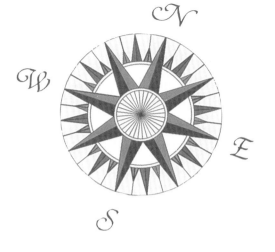

It was 1982 when I first became aware of Maine Windjammer Cruises. We were living in St. Croix, where Ann was working as a kindergarten teacher and I was captain in the local charter boat fleet. We had been drawn there seven years earlier, shortly after graduating from college, by my desire to sail and an interesting offer to Ann from the Virgin Islands Department of Education. We seemed to be settling in, buying a home and starting a family, but all that changed when I received a tattered copy of *Wooden Boat* Magazine, which arrived six months overdue.

On the cover was one of Camden's windjammers. I quickly searched for the feature story, 10 pages of pictures and text that I read twice before putting down the magazine. I was captivated by this charming coastal village seemingly filled with magnificent vessels from another century. The final page was a listing of all the windjammers with their owner's names and addresses. Was this article written just for me? I couldn't have dreamt of a more idyllic setting or way of life. That evening I put together a résumé and cover letters, and they went into the mail the very next day.

Before I knew it I was signed aboard a 95-foot schooner out of St. Thomas that was headed to New England for their summer season. This was just a reconnaissance mission to explore employment possibilities, secure housing and buy a vehicle. During my four days in Camden I met with all of the windjammer owners, rented a house a short walk from the harbor and bought an old but reliable station wagon.

Several of the owners said they would hire me if I was able to start right away. My reply was always, "I can't, but I'll be back in one month, ready, willing and able to take the first opportunity to sail aboard a windjammer." "Come see me when you get back," they said, "and we'll see what's

what." Captain Bex encouraged me to come see him first, and said, "If you're going to work for anyone around here, you might as well work for me, because I'm the only one who hires captains." This seemed like good advice, since all the other vessels were sailed by their owners.

Returning to St. Croix, there was a lot to do in the month before Ann finished school: wrapping up business affairs; dozens of projects on our home before we turned it over to renters; and saying farewell to our many friends. The time passed quickly. We were moving to Camden, Maine, "Windjammer Capital of the World."

The day after we arrived I went straight to the waterfront to see Captain Bex. "You're back," he said, and offered me a job on the spot. He apologized that the only berth available was as deckhand for $60 a week, but it was mine if I wanted it. Used to starting at the bottom, I jumped at the opportunity.

I was assigned to the *Mattie*, a 100-year-old veteran of the coasting trade. Going below to stow my gear in the fo'c'sle, I saw where the sailors who had entered here before me had worn the decks at the entrance to the scuttle. I thought of their voyages to the West Indies and along the coast. I thought of their work, the storms, the dangers they faced and the adventures they must have had. I realized I was about to become one of them, sleeping in the same berth, hauling on the same halyards and experiencing my own adventures, working aboard this magnificent tall ship.

There was a lot to learn that first season: the workings of the schooner, the waters of Penobscot Bay and the operations of the business. I suppose it went reasonably well, as Captain Bex offered me a captain's berth for the following summer. The mighty *Mistress*, our company's smallest schooner, was something of a toy compared to the bigger windjammers, but she was mine. To compensate for the speed advantage their longer waterlines gave the bigger vessels, we were often the first underway and the last to anchor. I was going to see Penobscot Bay, and my passengers were infected with the same enthusiasm.

The next summer I was thrilled by the opportunity to be in command of the 80-foot *Mercantile*. With up to 26 guests and a crew of five, every week was an adventure. Convinced this was just about the greatest vacation a person could have, I wanted to commit to this occupation. At the end of the season I approached Captain Les about buying the *Mercantile*. We talked through the winter, and the next summer he agreed to sell, but only if I bought the whole fleet. This was definitely more than I was bargaining for, but thinking this might be our only opportunity, Ann and I decided to take the plunge.

That fall, in the midst of our final negotiations, *Mattie* was hauled for inspection. The Coast Guard deemed her unfit for service and revoked her certificate to carry passengers. We agreed to proceed with the purchase of the fleet if repairs would begin immediately. It took several months to raise the money and write up the contracts. Meanwhile the project seemed to grow tenfold. In early February 1986, with Les and Ann Bex holding the mortgage and the *Mattie* still on the railway, the fleet changed hands.

Work on *Mattie* continued until late June, with *Mercantile* and *Mistress* getting an early start. In order to have any hope of being successful we extended the season, which for the first time began on Memorial Day weekend. That year we sailed the *Mercantile* together as a family, with Ann working as a deckhand in order to learn the ropes. Our girls, Allysa and Kristi (then six and three) were aboard with their 16-year-old nanny. We had a great summer. When I threw the lines to *Mattie* as we came alongside after our last trip I remember saying to myself, "Well, at least we did it for one season."

Mercantile, which I thought to be in better condition than *Mattie*, was now due for her two-year dry-dock examination. I had budgeted $10,000 and a month in the fall for repairs. As it turns out we were at the yard all winter, spending about $100,000 rebuilding the forward third of the vessel. We returned to Camden to finish the interior, including an entire new galley. In the weeks before sailing we worked well past midnight seven days a week. Still, when the passengers arrived there was much to do. Aft, the passenger accommodations were neat as a pin and guests boarded as normal. Forward was another story. The electricity and plumbing were not functioning in the galley. Carpenters were knee deep in sawdust and we still had to install tables, counters and even the cook stove. Convinced we could not possibly be ready to sail the next day, passengers' conversations usually revolved around, "So, what are you going to do on your vacation?"

The next morning we served our guests breakfast on the *Mattie* as we bagged up the sawdust, hauled the band saw and other tools ashore and did a major clean up of the *Mercantile*'s galley. Trucks arrived with the tables, stove and other components, which were quickly installed, and we were underway in time to serve lunch. Having slept only about 20 hours in the past week, I was happy to drop the anchor in a quiet cove and say "goodnight." That summer Ann cooked and we all had a great time. The summer went by in a flash, and as I tossed the lines to *Mattie* on our final trip I laughed as I said, "Well, at least we did it for two seasons."

Mattie was now due for her next two-year dry-dock inspection. By this time the Coast Guard was not shy about demanding extensive work regardless of the costs. I knew the best thing to do would be a total restoration, but that was not possible. Remembering our experience two years before, we expected that the patching the Coast Guard would require would cost more than we could hope to earn in a season or even two. This could go on forever and all we would have to show for our efforts would be two old boats full of patches. Sadly we surrendered the paperwork. We used the winter to regroup and develop a strategy that would allow us to do a complete and proper restoration of both our vessels. During our third season we operated only *Mercantile* and *Mistress*.

That fall I leased an abandoned shipyard and set it up for back-to-back restorations. There were a number of obstacles that had to be overcome at this location; first of all, there was no marine railway. We ran the *Mercantile* up on the beach on the high tide, releasing both anchors as we approached. Having attached floats to the chains' bitter ends, we would recover them later to pull us back out. As the tide went out a diver put blocking under the bilges to keep her upright. Working between the tides, we dug holes in the sand under the keel. A dozen 20-ton hydraulic jacks were employed to raise the schooner, slowly at first. The throw of the piston was about seven inches, but the weight of the vessel pushed the jacks down almost six inches into the wet ground, giving us a net gain of about an inch. Sliding shims in place, we regrouped and repeated the process, and slowly the schooner rose. When the *Mercantile* was about two feet off the ground we slid 10-inch I-beams under her to build a cradle. We used about 100 short pieces of pipe packed with concrete as rollers, and we borrowed some 1,700 feet of steel cable and huge blocks from a crane yard, making up a 10-part purchase. We pulled this with a large Caterpillar tractor; the tractor would pull down the beach for 100 feet and the schooner would inch ahead 10 feet. Slowly, we moved the schooner the 150 feet into the building.

When the schooner was in as far as it could go there was still about 30 feet sticking out of the building, so we built a large temporary extension with winged sheds to give us some protection from the cold winter months ahead. Les had a huge ship's saw, which he agreed to sell me. This all-important tool is a large tilting band saw; it allowed us to put a bevel in the massive timbers as we cut out the varied shapes.

The property still had some of the necessary machinery, including a 24-inch planer and a fully functioning belt-driven machine shop. Soon the retired machinist who had worked at the yard and was familiar with the shop showed up and offered his services. He had a soft spot for the *Mercantile*, because he had worked on her in his youth, during the '40s. Several other retired shipwrights familiar with this type of work joined the crew. With their guidance, our gang of young sailors and boat builders was ready to take on the job.

The repairs to the bow two years earlier gave us a good head start, but fully two thirds of the vessel remained to be rebuilt. The *Mattie* was still out of service, so it was important to get the *Merc* sailing. As expected, come spring we were behind schedule, and the first trip we sailed with only about eight cabins finished. Each week when we returned to Camden I would go to the office to see how many passengers we had scheduled for the next trip. Then I would grab my toolbox and head on board to finish the necessary cabins. It felt great to be sailing again.

Meanwhile, the *Mattie* was hauled the day after the *Merc*'s launching. The yard crew never missed a beat. Right about this time the *Mistress* hit a ledge in the Fox Islands Thorofare and was hauled at a yard in North Haven. The first report said it would take several weeks to repair the damage. The next day the yard manager called and said the damage was more serious than his initial look had revealed. It would take a minimum of 10 weeks to complete the work. As soon as the *Mercantile* was tied up in her berth that week I took the yawl boat over to North Haven. We put a temporary patch on the *Mistress* and had her launched so we could tow her to our yard in Rockland. The crew was waiting, and they went to work on her immediately. She was back in service the following week.

The restoration of the *Mattie* was a labor of love. As we dismantled her we found that she had an amazing amount of original wood, probably due to Edwin Bailey's access to the finest materials. We carefully removed the oak paneling from the main cabin to be reinstalled after the structure was rebuilt. Behind it we found newspapers dated 1882, telling of ship launchings and other important news of the day. These had been used as some kind of lining. Removing a house trunk that had been built to cover a passenger accommodation, we discovered the framework of the original cargo hatch. The remnants of many original details that had been covered up or lost during lesser repairs were also found. All these details would be incorporated into the newly restored schooner.

I felt it was important to do the restoration as accurately as possible and instructed the crew, "If you take out an oak 8x10, replace it with an oak 8x10. If you remove a yellow pine 4x8, replace it with the same." This wasn't always easy, and in one case it presented a huge challenge. The construction technique used in the *Mattie* called for more than 100 hanging and lodging knees. These L-shaped timbers secured the deck of the vessel to the hull. In the old days of shipbuilding these timbers were considered special, and were sought after by woodsmen. Other, less labor-intensive construction techniques have replaced this system, and today's industrial forestry makes it impossible to order such materials. I was advised to abandon the knee system and instead use a clamp-and-shelf arrangement that is standard for vessels built during the past 100 years.

Of course this would not do, so I had to find 100 hackmatack knees. I remembered reading a *Wooden Boat* Magazine interview with an old timer Down East who had made it his specialty to find such timbers. He was 83 years old and still going strong. When asked how long he might continue, the final quote in the article said, "Just as long as I can walk. As long as I can get around." That old-fashioned Yankee determination was just the attitude I needed, so I jumped in the truck and started driving. I brought the magazine with me, thinking I would read the article over one more time so that I would seem more knowledgeable on the subject when we spoke. Shortly before arriving at his house, I stopped to read and I smiled for a moment when I got to that last line. Suddenly I panicked. I flipped to the cover and saw that the magazine in my hand was exactly 10 years old. My old timer was 93!

The elderly woman who answered the door brought me to a room, where he sat motionless in a chair and stared out into the midday sun. He listened to my story as I explained my problem about the knees. He just turned to his wife and said, "Call the boy."

The "boy," it turned out, was his 62-year-old son, who had helped him for many years in the woods. The youngster agreed to help, but because of his full-time job he would only commit to half the number of knees I needed. He said the ground would freeze before he could harvest that many trees. He suggested that I harvest the remaining 50 knees myself and took me into the woods and explained the process. The knee is shaped from the root of the hackmatack. Unlike most trees, the hackmatack has no tap root that goes straight down. The roots spread out at almost 90 degrees as they grow just under the surface. The trick is to expose the roots, select the best and biggest one, and then saw it off at the appropriate length. Then, sawing the remaining roots close to the tree will cause it to fall. With the tree on the ground the trunk can be cut, producing the L-shaped timber.

We spent the next few weeks in the woods hunting knees. We managed to fell the trees, but they were much too heavy to carry out of the woods, so we returned to the project and kept working at the yard. Meanwhile, our friend Down East called to say his knees were ready to be picked up. The next day a young helper and I showed up in Baby Blue, my '51 Chevy flatbed, and loaded the knees. It was quite a load for the two-ton truck, but in an hour or two we were on our way. On the way home it started to snow and the roads were getting slippery. I found myself moving a little too fast down a steep hill in Bucksport. I just touched the breaks, but with all that weight she didn't want to slow down and we started to swerve. As I turned the wheel one way and then the other to try to get control, I shouted, "Hold on!" Somehow we managed to stay upright and on the road. With my heart pounding, I pulled over to regain my composure and said, "That was close." My young helper just turned and said, "Yeah, all I could see was us having to reload all those knees." Within three or four weeks there was plenty of snow, so we returned to the woods with a toboggan and pulled out our additional 50 knees. *Mattie* would be restored as original.

About this time, I received a phone call from James Delgado, the chief maritime historian for the National Park Service. He was conducting a survey of vessels that were considered of National Historic significance, their condition and any threat to their survival. When I told him we were in the middle of restoring the *Mattie* he was full of questions. He wanted to be sure we were as accurate as possible in our efforts. I told him he didn't have to worry about that, and started telling him about the knees. I felt it was an important detail, as I wasn't sure it still existed in any other vessel. His response was, "I can think of two: the USS *Constitution* and the USS *Constellation*." To that I replied, "Well, at least we are in good company."

Jim came to see the project with a photographer from the Park Service. It was a great compliment when he was quoted later in *Historic Preservation* Magazine describing our work: "They are some of the finest ship restorations I've ever seen." A short time later our schooners were among the first vessels from his survey to be recognized by the United States Congress as National Historic Landmarks.

Months before launching, the activity picked up to a rapid pace in hopes of completion on time, but as the months became weeks, it seemed only a dream. We continued to work; two shifts seven days a week, and I was there for all of them. If we were not going to be successful it wasn't because we weren't trying. Just when it seemed impossible, an old friend stopped by. He was a shipwright and said he'd heard I might need a hand. Boy did I, and I put him right to work. That next day another friend, one who had built his own schooner, came in carrying his toolbox and said he could work nights and weekends. Each day our crew grew as carpenters, riggers, painters and just good friends showed up to do whatever they could.

On Friday, June 29, 1990, two large Caterpillars dragged the schooner in her cradle down the beach. In a few hours she would float with the tide, a brand-new 108-year-old windjammer. Watching the tide rise can be a little boring, and we had a few other things to do, so everyone kept on working. One guy started a pool to see who would guess when she would float. Before we knew it someone noticed that she was moving, and we all took a pause as Ann cracked a bottle of champagne across her bow and rechristened her "*Grace Bailey*."

The crane had already arrived as we brought the *Grace* to a spot where we could get alongside the wharf at high tide to step the masts. Riggers rigged and caulkers caulked. Painters, varnishers, plumbers and mechanics of all trades worked feverishly, as passengers would arrive in only 48 hours! The owner of a large excursion boat that rented a berth on the wharf offered to let me tie up alongside to continue working. In a short while a police officer showed up and said the mayor wanted to see me. I was a bit busy to take time for congratulations, but it *was* the mayor. Chauffeured by the officer, I felt a bit awkward in my dirty overhauls as I entered the mayor's office, but I was shocked to find the real reason she'd summoned me. It appears that there must have been some dispute between the owner of the excursion boat and the city with respect to his use of the berth. His giving me permission to tie alongside was unacceptable. I had to leave the city-owned berth first thing in the morning.

On Saturday morning, the tide was high enough for us to return to the spot where we had stepped the masts the evening before. As soon as we had enough water we brought the *Grace* back around to the end of the wharf. As truckloads of pots and pans, mattresses, blankets and every conceivable thing we would need to set up a schooner for service came aboard, our friendly police officer stopped by. "I thought you were told to get out of here," he barked. I replied, "I have gotten away from the town berth that you rented to the captain. Why is it a problem that my schooner lies at a public waterfront in a spot that can't be utilized by anyone anyway, since there is no water at low tide?" To this he responded, "I have orders to put you under arrest if you're not off city property by 10:00 AM." I looked at my watch; it was 9:30.

Meanwhile, Baby Blue was backing up with all of our sails, running rigging, life rafts and other essential deck gear. Working as fast as we could, we piled the contents of the truck onto *Grace*'s deck. When the last item was aboard I looked at my watch, and it was one minute to 10. By now a considerable crowd had assembled, and I could see our officer with his arms folded, rocking back and forth on his heels. "Cast off the lines," I hollered, and in that moment of climax, there was silence, as the *Grace Bailey* floated inches from city property. "Keep working," was all I could say, and the crew stayed busy clearing the mess that had just come aboard, as I thought about what to do next.

Fortunately there was no wind, and we weren't going anywhere anyway, so we just drifted there while we cleared the decks and got organized enough to get underway. When I finally started the yawl boat someone from the dock shouted, "Where will you go?" "The fish pier," I replied. The manager was a friend of mine and I knew he would welcome me. When I got to the fish pier, a friendly gentleman caught my lines. I was surprised when he said, "You can't stay here." "Charlie's a friend of mine," I answered. "He won't mind."

"Charlie doesn't own the pier," he said, "it is city property and everyone including the officer heard you say you were coming here." "What about O'Hara's?" the man suggested. "Of course," I

replied. My new friend drove me to the fish plant, where Frank O'Hara was happy to help. And he owned the property. Somehow I managed to sneak back aboard my schooner and slip away without getting arrested, and I never heard from any Rockland city official again.

Ann drove a large crew belowdecks, organizing the galley and setting up the cabins for the guests scheduled to arrive the next day. On deck, our shrouds hung slack and the pile of canvas, spars and rigging that would propel the *Grace* just needed to be set up. Standing rigging, running rigging, spars and then sails; nothing could be simpler. But everything takes time, and when the passengers arrived we still were not ready. Fortunately Ann was doing a lot better job than I was, and she had all the cabins ready. She even baked cookies for our guests when they came aboard.

"What do you expect me to do?" cried a 75-year-old woman on the dock, looking up the steep ladder at low tide. It reminded me of early photographs of the schooners along the wharfs in Camden before boarding ramps. "Don't worry, Mattie," I said to our favorite longtime passenger, who first sailed on the *Mattie* in 1939. "We'll get you aboard." We set up the boson's chair and brought her aboard in grand style.

The new passenger accommodations were far more comfortable. All of the dormitory-style cabins were gone. Each new cabin was private, with a double bed or two singles. There were heads located in each passenger area and we even added a hot shower, which was unheard of when I'd arrived eight years earlier. A spacious new galley allowed everyone to eat together, unlike the former arrangement where food was brought to the smaller main cabin where we ate in shifts. Things were looking up at Maine Windjammer Cruises.

The projects that followed were small by comparison. When we decided to rebuild the *Mistress* at our new shop we didn't even start until January. She was always a little tight and not a great sailor because of her blunt transom. To compensate for this we lengthened her out by eight feet and added a lead-ballast keel. Her fine new counter rose gracefully out of the water to her new transom, and her rig grew as well. She is now a fine sailor and more comfortable at the same time.

We spent another winter remasting the schooners. A trip to Oregon located huge Douglas firs, which were transported to Maine for final shaping. We made two masts and a new bowsprit for the *Mercantile* and a complete new rig for the *Grace Bailey*. Using old photographs, we recreated her original headrig, crafting a new bowsprit and jibboom. With these changes and a new set of sails she was a joy to sail, perfectly balanced, as I knew she would be.

I felt my work was complete, but that is never the case when owning three large wooden schooners. There is always something that needs to be done. Those early years were certainly challenging and the reward was simply to have lived them. For the most part, the less tumultuous years that followed the restorations have been filled with grand sailing adventures for our family, shared with thousands of guests whose participation has been "Keeping the Tradition Alive."

Three Schooners Sold To Captain Of *Mercantile*

by Liz Soloway   (Camden Herald 1986)

Three of Camden's prized schooners – the *Mattie*, the *Mercantile* and the *Mistress* – have made Raymond Williamson a very happy man. After four years of working on the schooners, previously owned by Captain Les Bex, Williamson and his wife Ann have bought the fleet of three.

"I never thought this would happen," said Williamson, who first heard of Camden's Windjammers in an article in Wooden Boat magazine. "I saw the *Mary Day* on the cover, read the article, and sent letters to all the owners, asking if they had a job for me," Williamson recalled. That was in the spring of 1982. By June, he was working for Captain Bex on the 81 ft. *Mattie*. Williamson moved on to become captain of the 46-foot *Mistress* in 1983, and served as captain of the 80-foot *Mercantile* in 1984.

"I approached Bex after my first season on the *Mercantile* with the idea of buying it," Williamson said. Bex, however, did not want to break up the fleet and asked Williamson to consider purchasing all three of the vessels. After his second season on the *Mercantile*, Williamson decided to take Bex up on his offer.........................

HI HO
HAPPY HOLIDAYS
and
Best Wishes
for the
NEW YEAR!

Grace Bailey and Mercantile

In their berth at the Public Landing in Camden

Photograph: Fred LeBlanc

The Williamsons Begin Their Watch

Photograph: *Camden Herald*

Courtesy of Maine Windjammer Cruises

Mercantile Bow Rebuild

Collection: Maine Windjammer Cruises

Mercantile

With new bow, hauled out to complete her restoration

Collection: Capts. Douglas K. & Linda J. Lee

Mattie

Just before haul out for restoration

Collection: Maine Windjammer Cruises

Mattie

Undergoing restoration

Photograph: Linda K. Serafin

Collection: Maine Windjammer Cruises

Ship's Saw

Hackmatack knees for *Mattie* in the background

Photograph: Candace Clifford, National Park Service

Collection: Maine Windjammer Cruises

Mattie

New knees in place

Photograph: Candace Clifford, National Park Service

Collection: Maine Windjammer Cruises

Mattie

More knees

Photograph: Candace Clifford, National Park Service

Collection: Maine Windjammer Cruises

Williamson Family

The early years

Collection: Maine Windjammer Cruises

Mattie Mosher

Our favorite long-time passenger

Collection: Maine Windjammer Cruises

Schooner Mercantile

Photograph: Neal Parent

Sunset

Viewed from the *Grace Bailey*

Photograph: Fred LeBlanc

Collection: Maine Windjammer Cruises

Grace Bailey

Camden Hills in the background

Photograph: Fred LeBlanc

Collection: Maine Windjammer Cruises

Mercantile
Passing Butter Island
Photograph: Fred LeBlanc
Collection: Maine Windjammer Cruises

Grace Bailey and Mercantile
Photograph: Fred LeBlanc
Collection: Maine Windjammer Cruises

Mercantile
A hazy day
Photograph: Fred LeBlanc
Collection: Maine Windjammer Cruises

Grace Bailey
Quiet cove on a misty morning
Photograph: Fred LeBlanc
Collection: Maine Windjammer Cruises

Mercantile and Grace Bailey
Setting out from Camden Harbor
Photograph: Robert Jenks
Collection: Maine Windjammer Cruises

Mercantile
Photograph: Jan Burnham
Collection: Maine Windjammer Cruises

Grace Bailey
Photograph: George Borne

Grace Bailey
Great Schooner Race
Photograph: Barbara Hatch
Collection: Maine Windjammer Cruises

Mercantile
Photograph: © Benjamin Mendlowitz

Schooner Grace Bailey
Front Cover Photo
Photograph: Neal Parent

Mistress
Photograph: © Benjamin Mendlowitz

Mistress
Photograph: © Benjamin Mendlowitz

Mercantile
Quiet anchorage
Photograph: Fred LeBlanc
Collection: Maine Windjammer Cruises

Mercantile
A picture-perfect day
Photograph: Fred LeBlanc
Collection: Maine Windjammer Cruises

Mistress and Grace Bailey
Photograph: Fred LaBlanc
Collection: Maine Windjammer Cruises

Schooner Mistress
Photograph: Fred LeBlanc
Collection: Maine Windjammer Cruises

Underway Aboard the Grace Bailey
Captain Ray at the helm
Photograph: Barry King
Collection: Maine Windjammer Cruises

Grace Bailey
Charging ahead
Back Cover Photo
Photograph: Ted Dillard

The Williamson Family
Working together
Collection: Maine Windjammer Cruises

Captain Ray and Ann
Photograph: Don Pizzuto

Maine Windjammer Cruise's Passengers
Our valued cargo that loads itself
Collection: Maine Windjammer Cruises

Schooner Mistress
Photograph: Fred LeBlanc
Collection: Maine Windjammer Cruises

Grace Bailey
Through the *Mercantile*'s rigging
Photograph: Fred LeBlanc
Collection: Maine Windjammer Cruises

Mercantile
Eggemoggin Reach
Photograph: Fred LeBlanc
Collection: Maine Windjammer Cruises

The Fleet
Grace Bailey, Mercantile and *Mistress*
Photograph: Robert Jenks
Collection: Maine Windjammer Cruises

The Fleet
Waiting for springtime
Photograph: Sara Ruffin